How to Maintain Healthy Hair at Home

Faith Haygood

Ahmed, A. (2016). 22 Amazing Benefits of Drinking Water for Skin, Hair and Health. [online] StyleCraze. Available at: https://www.stylecraze.com/.../benefits-of-water-for-skin-hair-and-health/ [Accessed 25 Nov. 2018]

ISBN: 1727732294
ISBN-13: 978-1727732290

TABLE OF CONTENT

<u>FOREWORD</u>

Brilliant, is how I would describe this masterpiece.

It's simply packaged, but a powerful read! You

will find "hair nuggets" that will assist you in

maintaining healthy hair at home, while you are

away from the Salon.

In her new book "How to Maintain Healthy Hair

at Home" Faith Haygood delivers professional

advice to your doorstep, without compromise of the

facts we all want to know.

Your Stylist will wonder how you've maintained

such healthy hair. I applaud Faith Haygood for

trailblazing the way, and even sharing industry

secrets. Often, these essential tools aren't shared

with clients. Well, not anymore! You'll find many

of your answers right here in this easy -to- read

manual. In my 20 plus years as a Cosmetologist, I've seen first hand the effects of bad hair care between hair services. The outcome can be life altering.

Faith Haygood has 15 plus years in the beauty industry, and many of those years I've worked closely with her. Faith is a leading expert in her field. She exhibits creativity, passion, and knowledge. I recommend every household to have at least one copy of this book at your fingertips. You'll find that this is a great go-to-manual.

"Finally, someone is taking the "charge" to teach us how to maintain healthy hair at home."

- Michelle K. Patterson, Cosmetologist

HAIR NUGGEST TOOL

At Home Must Haves:

Combs (Wide Tooth, Rat Tail, Detangler, and Feather)

Brush (Paddle, Vent, Boar, and Denman)

Blow Dryer (Hand Held and Hooded)

1-inch Flatiron (depending on your hair length)

Shampoo

Conditioner

Leave-in Conditioner

Bobby-pins

Oil (Coconut, Moroccan, or Argan)

Edge Control or Vitamin E Gel Capsule (For Loss Edges)

Ponytail Holders (No Rubber Bands)

Hair Nugget: You may or may not know how to use some of these tools just yet, but with a little practice you will get the hang of it.

<u>INTRODUCTION</u>

Have you ever left the salon looking and feeling like a million bucks, only to ask yourself this simple question once you made it home; "how do I maintain this style on my own?" These basic instructions that I like to refer to as "hair *nuggets*," will help you maintain healthy hair for you and your family in the comfort of your own home.

As a hairstylist for over 15 years, I've seen the good, bad, and the ugly when it comes to hair care. But the best part about this business is having the ability to provide a solution in this fast and growing industry. I am passionate about people becoming their best self from the inside out. I desire to help people be the best they can be. This book is one of the ways that I've decided to help others and give back.

I have compiled a step-by-step manual to ensure that proper hair maintenance is applied at home. Giving a haircut, color, or style is only half of the battle. Simple hair care routines at home and a frequent visit with your hair care professional, makes for a LIFETIME OF HEALTHY HAIR!

With the vast growing number of non-professionals on social media, hair care has taken a back seat, and a quick fix of the latest trends and styles seems to be more important than the hair attached to the scalp. Hair manufacturers are makings billions of dollars off the fact that some of us have become lazy with personal care and allowing weaves, braids, and wigs to hide our true glory-YOUR OWN HAIR. Don't get me wrong; I love the variety of wigs and weaves because it allows creativity, culture, and expression of one self to come alive. The problem that I want to address is not properly taking care of the hair underneath the installments. The basics like shampoo, conditioner and end trimming is must before braid. If there is a strong smell and you've had the style for a few months, it's time to take it down, out or off. Fungus can grow and cause serious health problems that cannot be handled by your stylist.

Hair Nugget: Maybe you don't wear weaves, braids, or wigs, but you can't seem to tame your unruly strands. I wrote this manual mainly for you. I will try to cover as much as possible, so you can be on your way to maintaining healthy hair.

HELP, MY HAIR IS STRESSED OUT

In my years of experience, I have learned how to use my five senses to understand the client's needs and offer suggestions. It's not always easy because people will not tell you the total truth, but the more you ask questions the more they begin to open up. Usually, 75% of what is diagnosed mentally is revealed. So how do you know if your hair is stressed out? First, your hair is stressed if your hair is very dry or it will not hold moisture. Second, if there is a lot of breakage while combing, your hair is stressed. Third, your hair is stressed if you don't take care of it.

This is understandable, especially if you have a busy lifestyle. However, your hair underneath weave and wigs should be your number one priority. Wearing wigs and braids might not be your story or you're a low maintenance kind of person, but you like wearing ponytails. If your hair is not growing and has been the same length for over a year, it might be stressed out. Remember, your hair should grow a half an inch every month.

Hair Nugget: A few simple ways you can measure your growth:

1.Create "hair history" with your stylist. He/she will be able to see your growth from a different angle.

2. Look at old pictures from the year before. Do you notice any differences?

3. Maintaining a healthy routine at home.

4. Don't beat yourself up if you have not done either of these tips. You can start right NOW and begin to see a positive change soon!

5. Set aside hair care expenses for the month. Just as a car needs routine maintenance to run properly, the

way you look, and feel is just as important.

WATER, VEGGIES, AND VITAMINS, OH MY!

Water

Yup! I know you felt it coming. You hear it on the news, social media, from your hairstylist, and your body. DRINK MORE WATER! According to "*StyleCraze,*" an online article entitled: "*22 Amazing Benefits of Drinking Water,*" written by Arshi Ahmed states: *"Water is a natural miracle ingredient that supports vitamin consumption and assists inefficient and healthy hair growth. Water makes almost ¼ of the weight of a hair strand, thus, drink two liters of water every day to get gleaming and healthy tresses."* Hair loves moisture. In fact, it longs for water, just like our body. If we don't stay hydrated, we become dizzy, have lack of energy, and/or feel fatigue. Our hair feels and negatively reacts to lack of water as well.

Veggies

Vegetables and fruit are packed with a lot of professional benefits that will help you maintain a healthy lifestyle. Everyone could benefit from ". mother nature." If you didn't know, here are some veggies and fruit that can promote hair growth: onions, sweet potatoes, spinach, and carrots just to name a few. Avocados also have multiple benefits, which includes: hair, nails and skin growth. Find fruits and vegetables that you like and implement them in your diet. As your appetite changes, so will your hair.

Vitamins

Okay I'm going to be honest, I do not take my vitamins like I should, but when I do take them on a daily base, I can see a tremendous difference in the texture of my hair. My hair has more shine, is more manageable, experience less breakage, plus I'm consuming more water when I take vitamins. You should try it. I have always recommended my clients to take biotin, vitamin E, vitamin D, Horsetail or silica.

Hair Nugget: Please consult with your doctor before taking any of the above-mentioned vitamins. If you are unsure about these vitamins that I mentioned, locate a local health food store and ask representatives any questions that you may have or research the benefits of the vitamins online. Vitamin intake today keeps damaging hair away and healthy hair is on its away.

THE GREENER THE GRASS

Some people love to see quick results. Hair care is not like using a microwave. You just can't pop it in for a second and it's done. You must allow the process of germination to take place within hair care. Like anything, hair care takes time to see results.

When getting my clients to see what I see, I like to use the analogy of green grass. The homeowner (you) may have a beautiful lawn. A person may admire how great your lawn (hair) looks, but the homeowner knows it didn't happen overnight. See, you must plant the right seeds making sure the soil is good, water the lawn, and keep it trimmed. Maintaining healthy hair may be a process, but the results are priceless.

Hair Nuggets:

1. The soil (The Scalp)

2. The fertilizer (Shampoo & Conditioner)

3. Water (Moisturize, Oil, Etc.)

4. Trim the lawn (TRIM THOSE ENDS)

THE RIGHT STUFF

Choosing the right product for your hair can be overwhelming, costly, and unfruitful if you don't know what to look for. Today's market for manufacturing products is changing every day, so it may be hard trying to figure out what truly works for you. I've heard countless stories from clients sharing how much money they've spent on products only to hear them say, "It didn't do anything for my hair." In some cases, companies spend plenty of time packaging the outside of the product, so it can be appealing to the consumer. However, the substance inside may be watered down ingredients that leave your hair in the same state as before- lifeless. The ONLY way to ensure you're getting the best for your buck is by setting an appointment for a consultation. The stylist will help guide you with understanding your hair needs.

Hair Nugget: Not all social media and YouTube videos are bad. But to be sure you're getting the personal attention you need; the safer way is to consult your stylist. Some first-time consultations are usually free. If not, you'll still walk away with some great hair nuggets and possibly a "goodie bag" to get you started.

<u>SQUEAKY CLEAN</u>

The most important part of a hairstyle is not the finished product. Seventy five percent of your style starts with a clean scalp. Shampooing the hair properly will remove dirt, oils, gels, and product build up. Once you've completely saturated the hair under the running water, you can now apply shampoo in hand. A quarter size should do. The first shampoo will not lather right away, but be patient, the second or third shampoo will produce the rich lather you desire. Use figure tips to massage the scalp. Rinse hair completely until water is clear.

Hair Nugget: Hair has a certain feel to it once it's clean. If it still feels clammy, don't be ashamed to shampoo one more time. Once your hair is squeaky clean, towel dry and move to the next step.

<u>IM BRINGING MOISTURE BACK</u>

After squeezing and towel blotting the hair from excess water, apply conditioner into your hand using a quarter size. Feel free to use a little more conditioner depending on length of the hair. **Here's a hair nugget secret**; because your hands still have conditioner on it, rub them together to activate heat and apply the rest of the conditioner on the hands to the hair, focusing on the ends. Repeat if necessary.

After you have applied conditioner, use a wide tooth comb (starting from the ends and work your way up to the roots) and comb until all the hair is combed out and free from tangles. Place a plastic cap on your head. After 5-10 minutes, rinse hair and apply leave-in conditioner.

Hair Nugget: Just because a product is labeled "Conditioning Shampoo" does not mean you should just shampoo only. Apply a cream conditioner and let it penetrate for 5- 10 minutes before moving to the next step. Once complete, rinse your hair in warm/cool water. Conditioners help restore moisture and prevent future breakage that result in split ends. Bringing moisture back will make the hair more manageable and prevent heat damage in the future.

RELAX, IT'S JUST HAIR

If you have relaxed hair and need a touch up, my suggestion would be to make an appointment with a licensed professional. A stylist can see the overall scope of the scalp and can properly apply relaxer accordingly. This will prevent over processing and/or choosing the wrong type of relaxer that is not for your hair type. If you choose to use a home kit from the drug store, always read the instructions given by the manufacture. I would hate for you to over-process and damage your beautiful strands.

Hair Nugget: In my opinion relaxers don't take out your hair, it's how you take care of your hair with a relaxer. Also, I would not recommend relaxers for anyone under 18 years of age. A teenager's hair is still maturing, and without proper care at home, it may cause breakage. We are almost

at the home stretch. Just know that I am so proud of

you! You are doing a great job following these

basic steps.

<u>BLOW DRYER AND THE HOOD</u>

Depending on the length of your hair, choose the correct brush for this process and you'll be done in no time. It might be easier to use a vent or paddle brush for medium to longer hair. A paddle brush is great for simulating the scalp and producing natural oils locked in the strands.

Set the temperature according to the texture of the hair. A hot setting cannot only burn strands but your scalp too, causing more damage to your hair. For shorter hair, molding the hair down with an "setting foam" and wraps will be your best friends for under the dyer. You might not want to sit for 20 minutes, but your goal should be healthy shiny dry hair, so go for it.

Hair Nuggets: For extra protection against

styling tools; once your hair is dry, apply a light oil,

and then comb your hair out. Proceed with desired

style.

<u>HOW TO CHOOSE A SUITABLE HAIR</u>

<u>STYLIST</u>

1. Consult a Licensed Professional for all your hair-care needs.

2. Choose a Stylist that is knowledgeable and skillful. This will help you achieve your desired outcome.

3. Be clear and concise about any hair care questions, concerns, and goals you may have. In other words, tell them everything about your hair.

4. Listen to your Stylist and discuss realistic objectives to help you achieve your short term and long-term goals.

5. Commit to your scheduled appointments and

remember to apply the hair care

maintenance tips provided in this manual.

Hair Nugget: Your stylist should be

passionate about giving you the best service. If you

feel uncomfortable for whatever reason, it's ok to

find someone else that fits your needs and budget.

<u>HAIR NUGGET DO'S AND DON'TS</u>

Do's:

1. Daily maintenance is important; your
hair will thank you.

2. Locate a suitable Stylist that
understands your hair care needs.

3. Take care of your body. Eat well, rest
and drink plenty of water.

Don'ts

1. Never pull or tug on the hair while
detangling. A wide tooth comb or paddle
brush   should do the trick.

2. Never mix colors, relaxers and any other
chemicals together without product
knowledge. You may cause severe damage
to the scalp or baldness.

3. Don't ever be afraid to ask your hair care
professional questions. If they are unsure,
trust, they'll find an answer.

Hair Nugget: Take the time and enjoy life and the simple things around you. You'll be glad you did.

You can maintain healthy hair just by knowing what works best for your hair. Although there are many resources on the web, like YouTube and Pinterest, allow a professional the opportunity to give you a personal advice and stick with one or two stylist that knows your **hair history**. All hair types are not the same but having hair that is healthy is the same method. Allow the product to work as instructed by the manufactures. With anything, it takes time to see results. Remember the grass?

1. The soil (the scalp)

2. The fertilizer (shampoo & conditioner)

3. Water (moisturize, oil, etc.)

4. Trim the lawn (TRIM THOSE ENDS)

NATURAL AND RELAXED: HOW OFTEN SHOULD I TRIM MY ENDS?

Listen people; your hairstylist is not out to get you. It's not a sin to trim those ends! No matter what walk of life you are from, it is essential to the process of hair growth. Remember these points:

1. The hair grows ½ a month; the longer you wait, the more damage you can cause to your hair. The wind, pillow, excessive combing, over processed hair (color and relaxer), rubber bands, wools hats, and even coats can assist with damaging your hair.

2. Splitting ends causes damage and eventually more hair may need trimming during the hair service due to your hair trim being prolonged.

3. Let a professional trim your ends. A stylist should not only trim, but also color and relax your hair too.

<u>HOW DO I GET RID OF DANDRUFF?</u>

No one wants to have dandruff in their hair.

Dandruff can be caused by having dry skin, your

hair being sensitive to certain products, or/and

specific skin conditions. Here are a few tips to help

get rid of dandruff:

1. Use a dandruff shampoo.

2. Drink plenty of water

3. Get deep conditioner service often. once a
   month.

4. Dispel hair myth.

Hair Nugget: Do not put oil on your scalp.

Putting oil/grease on the scalp, coats the scalp,

clogged pores and prevents dandruff from lifting off

scalp. Place oil on the strands for overall coverage.

<u>HOW TO REMOVE GLUE AND PREVENT DAMAGE</u>

DOES HAIR GLUE DAMAGE HAIR? YES OR NO

Here are some big No, No's!

1. Too much glue!

2. Pulling/snatching weave out

3. Constantly regluing the same section to maintain a style longer. This can be damaging, especially around the edges/ hairline.

Hair Nugget: Instead, remove glue this way:

1. Shampoo hair… run water until loosen. 2-3mins

2. Apply shampoo as you would your own hair.

3. Focus on the weft of weave by using finger tips. Repeat first step.

4. Use cream conditioner, wide tooth comb to remove excess glue.

5. Repeat steps to ensure all glue is removed.

6. Make routine appointments with your hair professional.

<u>STYLING AND PROFILING</u>

Most people find it difficult when it comes to styling their own hair. Listen, I understand, which is why you need a reliable stylist to help guide you when you're in between services. Every style has the basic elements designed by your stylist for you to maintain your style at home.

A cut, color, weave, or even braids have simple rules for maintenance. All you have to do is ask your stylist, follow these hair nuggets, and begin to see the results you want to see.

Hair Nugget: Changing your diet can also decrease hair loss and increase the nutrition you need for healthy looking hair. I hope I have answered some of your hair care concerns. My desire is that everyone will understand how to maintain healthy hair at home. If I accomplished

that, then I have done well.